OUR PERFECT CHAOS

A POETIC DIALOGUE BETWEEN AN ADULT DAUGHTER AND HER MOM

TIERRA BANKS

OUR

PERFECT CHAOS

A poetic dialogue between an

adult daughter and her mom

TIERRA BANKS

ISBN 978-1-7360594-0-1 print

ISBN 978-1-7360594-1-8 e-book

Cover by Intelligent Design

Author photo by JG Photography

Printed in the United States

For more information please email the author at

tierrabanks@mendedinc.org

www.mendedrelationships.com

Follow Tierra or her organization on social media

@tierradbanks @mendedinccle

To Peyton, this one is for you. May our story be
different, not perfect but progressive.
Let's love each other for all our lives!

To my beautiful mother Willette, thank you for giving me
everything you had, including your permission to share
our story. I love you so much and I am forever
blessed to call you Mommy!

CONTENTS

Preface 1

Mother Wound 7

This Ain't Normal 10

Maturation 14

The Basement 16

When the Plan Failed 19

The Thin Line 22

I'm so Full 25

My Teacher 29

Just Stop 31

Daydreaming 34

Let Me Explain 36

My Daughter, My Gift 38

What I Wanted Ain't What I Got 42

My Reflection 45

Dear Momma 47

Her Cup Runneth Empty 50

I Can Handle the Truth 53

So, You Want the Truth Huh? 55

Her-Story 59

That's It...I'm Throwing It Away 62

A Teacher Indeed 65

It Could Be Worse 69

Apology..72

Love Like Candy 75

Thinking out loud................................78

In Hindsight................................81

Taking Credit................................83

Spears Shaken 86

My Momma Cold................................89

I Am Needy 92

A Mother 95

We'll Get There 98

I'm Proud of You................................101

Communication 104

Stamp of approval 107

Framework 111

I'm changing 115

Final Thoughts 119

PREFACE

Hey Sis,

My name is Tierra Banks, and I am a wife, mother, daughter, sister, aunt, friend, mentor, mentee, coach, social worker and founder of Mended Inc- a nonprofit committed to restoring broken mother-daughter relationships worldwide! I know- I know, we are always defining ourselves by the titles we have, so forgive me, because those things aren't at all who I am. My reason for revealing my roles was to shine light on the fact that my relationship with my mother has deeply influenced my relationships with everyone else involved in my life. Quite frankly, that's a lot of people who may have been affected by my brokenness.

To all those who knew me before I decided to heal, I APOLOGIZE. From the bottom of my heart, I am sorry for being co-dependent, messy, immature, annoying, hurtful, selfish, weak, inconsiderate, uncompassionate and disrespectful. For years I bled on many people, blaming my circumstances instead of taking charge of my life. Today, I call a spade a spade. I've been through some stuff! I own that and have decided to walk in my truth, move forward with my purpose and use my story as a tool to help you do the same! We are overcoming every day!

You see, I was raised by a motherless daughter. For as long as I could remember, I would hear stories of how my grandmother was murdered in Chicago while visiting her dad. As a child, it was only a sad story to me; one that reminded me of creepy unsolved mystery shows, but nothing that I ever lost sleep over. Back then, I had no idea how to define or identify trauma. I had no clue my mom had experienced a traumatic event. I thought over time she had gotten over it since she no longer cried when telling the story. I knew the story carried sentimental value because of how carefully my mom stored the tattered clothing my grandmother wore the night she was killed. But I had no clue she was hurting my entire life!

The disconnect in our relationship occurred much later than my birth, but far too early in my formative years. While I was cognitively developing, my mother was emotionally deteriorating. I needed her in ways I could not articulate, and she had given of herself for as long as she could. Throughout that time our communication became dangerous. We pierced each other's hearts with words sharp enough to destroy everything. We viewed each other as enemies, whose mere existence was unsettling, and we both just wanted out!

Our relationship remained critical and sensitive for the next several years. We experienced trial after trial, devastation after devastation. Our family grew through marriage and adoption, we grieved the death of loved ones, we superficially celebrated each other's accomplishments; all while ignoring our real issues. According to us our broken relationship was normal; what was there to work through? Of course, some things we experienced were typical "mom/daughter" stuff, but some weren't. Then, there were other situations that only stung as bad as they did because we chose to deal alone.

That is why I decided to obey God and publish this book. The purpose of *Our Perfect Chaos* is to provide hope, healing and help to every mother and daughter who's ever struggled in this sacred relationship. Initially I asked myself, "Why write short stories and poems?", then I thought, "Why not?". Parables (simple stories) were often used in the bible by Jesus, so that the people could understand. I'm following His lead using our story.

My prayer is that you are inspired enough to begin your own healing journey. I hope that as you read, you gain understanding of some of the choice's mom made that may not have been considerate of you. I also hope that compassion and empathy (for yourself and mom) flood your heart as you travel down memory lane. My greatest hope is for you to begin healthy and balanced conversations, with a goal to understand each other wholly. Ideally, both of you will become inquisitive about your individual stories. I hope you become compelled to share vulnerably, accept the past for what it was, respect each other's perspective, and forgive one another completely! I know I make it sound way too easy! My goal is to simplify the possibility of restoration. God wants you to be whole! It really is hard work-but being apart can be even harder.

For best results, I recommend that you continue the conversation with a professional counselor and mentor or friend! Some memories may surface that are too painful to disclose to mom or daughter right away, if this occurs, simply become aware of how you feel, record your emotions, reflect on how you were affected, and decide what steps you must take to heal.

Then proceed to share if or when you are comfortable. Remember, the purpose of this book is to prompt action; whatever you do, don't forget why you started!

Happy Healing,

Tierra Banks 🖤

"He heals the brokenhearted and

binds up their wounds"

-Psalm 147:3

MOTHER WOUND

This wound I have can't be bandaged

It won't heal with stitches or tape or any other thing in the medicine cabinet

The first aid kit ain't equipped to wipe away this hurt

It's a deep cut, so deep that it continues to ooze year after year

It's infected too

I know because I watch everyone who encounter it become sick

Their smiles begin to resemble my frown the longer they stay

This wound of mine can't be handled in a quick trip to the doctor

Especially not the one I'm willing to be seen by

Maybe the kind that have a couch in their exam room could help me

But where I'm from, we don't believe in therapy

I'm running out of options

My wound is too thick

It demands all types of attention- medical, mental, and miraculous

It needs to be understood so that it can be healed

So that the poison is no longer venomous, and the stench no longer hypnotizes

It needs God

But then I heard Him say…

Then give me the wound

"A lie doesn't become truth, wrong doesn't become right & evil doesn't become good, just because it's accepted by the majority"

-unknown

THIS AIN'T NORMAL

I recall a day where I was fed up with you. You had been yelling and complaining about how junky we were. You went on and on about how you were tired of cleaning up after us. Somehow your rant became never ending. It went from our junkiness to our ungratefulness then ended up with how you never wanted kids anyway.

Before that day I was numb to your tantrums. I had memorized when and what would make you tick. But that time was different, it was something about how you looked that made me believe every word you said. The daggers you were throwing began to cut; "Maybe we were as trifling as you claimed" I thought. Maybe we didn't deserve the luxurious bunk beds and second-hand clothes we had. Whatever the case, my mind became tormented as you repeatedly screamed insults.

I flipped. I will never forget how surprised you looked as I, your "good kid" read you your rights. Now, I'm not proud of that at all but I had to do what I had to do. My womanhood was threatened. Yeah, I was only sixteen, but I was going through some things. I was trying my best to help bear your burden by working and contributing to bills. I was doing laundry and cleaning up after you and your new man. I even would cook dinner when you were too tired to do it, so I couldn't let you disrespect me like I was some amateur.

Now that I'm grown with my own kids to raise, I see how disrespectful my response was and until now I justified it because so was yours. My daughter and I recently had an argument and before I realized, I had transformed into that same monster you became about fourteen years ago. As we went back and forth, I felt my heart breaking as I watched my baby girl shrink.

She couldn't out do me with her words, I had been trained by the best!

Suddenly she burst into tears. While part of me felt as though I had conquered this tiny giant, the other part of me felt like the coward I was portraying. For the first time, I sincerely apologized immediately to my daughter. I had to explain how the little girl in me had gained control of my tongue. It was almost like I could not believe what I had become, especially because I always said I'd never be like that. But there I was, running on fumes and spitting fire on those I loved dearly.

That's when I decided to work on me, because contrary to popular belief, that wasn't normal. And in my home, that type of dysfunction will never be okay.

"There's a critical moment when the daughter suddenly real-
izes that the mother is another woman. Before that,
a mother is a symbol. She's all knowing, all powerful,
maybe the enemy and maybe a nurturer- but you
don't see her as another woman with
similar problems & experiences"

-unknown

MATURATION

Cute, little, sassy, pink

Growing, molding, connecting, link

Highschool, boys, jobs, clothes

Pain, purpose, friends, foes

Lessons, whippings, grounded, talks

Hate, confusion, embarrassment, hawk

Wisdom, apologies, acceptance, mature

Trust, honor, respect, and more

"It shouldn't hurt to be a child"

-D. P. Babin

THE BASEMENT

The basement's dark and wet walls echoed secrets as the years went by. They offered no escape for those trapped by the jeepers creepers who crept down there and waited for the innocent to wander. She thought she was safe because the ranger was guarding the park but the ranger slipped away and so he slipped his hands in her pants.

Those damn basement walls were no park. No ranger was there, but the monster was still lurking. He played with the innocent fibers of her youth with his fingers. Manipulated her mind with his game. Tortured her with thoughts that has trapped her for years- "A man is always in control" he said. She laid there and stared into space as her tiny A cups were ripped apart by the fangs of the monster masked as a protector. The creepiness of his voice programed worthlessness and weakness into her soul.

All the while, her mind wondered where the ranger was. How did she not feel what the basement walls were hosting? A birthing of pain and pity, of depression and shame. Poor baby girl had to lie as a virgin to not appear fast and be stripped of her dignity in a blink of an eye. Her body went numb because feeling good was not an option. She had felt pleasure before, but this…this was nasty! It was disgusting and gut-wrenching. Imagine being violated by a beast who was big and mean with shattered teeth.

The agony and despair from that night smothered her. The ridicule from what happened scarred her. The smells, the dark, the stairs all reminded her and every time she heard similar words to what the monster said…she clung to them. It's like she forgot what she said she wouldn't remember. His lies, her own demons, and the rangers blame all weakened her. It all started in that damn basement.

"Me too"

Tarana Burke

WHEN THE PLAN FAILED

Baby did I ever tell you that I was molested too? Sure was. My virginity was taken from me when I was just eight. By the time I was fourteen I had been penetrated three times, all by men I had to live with. That stuff had me so messed up, I decided to start giving my goodies away. I'm surprised I don't have more kids or some burning sensation that I can't get rid of. Thanks be to God.

When you and your sister were born, I vowed that I would kill a "you know what", if they touched y'all. I bought a nice 38 just in case something popped off. I had a rehearsed speech prepared for the violator too. Nobody; and I meant nobody, was going to inflict such horrible things on my two. I have never been the same since I came out the basement, so I knew what it felt like. They would have to kill me if I couldn't kill them, cuz I planned to take from them every ounce of peace they took from y'all if they tried it!

But then they tried it and at that moment I realized I was already dead. Spiritual death had taken me some years before it happened. I was dead the day I shopped for my gun. So much of my attention went to how I would handle the situation that I forgot to prevent it. I instantly became someone else. It was like watching the same movie but in a different theater. Somehow, I thought that the change of scenery would change the outcome. I thought that having good intentions was enough. Nobody had pulled a gun on anyone for me. Nobody confronted the pedophile like I did!

You were a mature kid, so I even asked you baby what you wanted to do about it. I was willing to do whatever you wanted, it just had to be your choice. And when you chose differently than I felt like I would have if I were in your shoes, I stopped believing you. My mind told me that a hurt girl would have wanted to make him pay but you didn't and in turn I made you pay.

21

"A mother's love for her child is like nothing else in the world. It knows no law, no pity, it dares all things, and it crushes down remorselessly all that stands in its path."

Agatha Christie

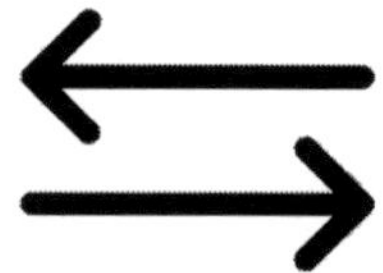

THE THIN LINE

There's such a thin line between love and hate.

So yes, I hate that I can't be the mother you dreamt I would be

And yes, I do hate that you respect other women more than me

I hate how no matter how many times I apologize for the past, you always bring it back up

I hate that you think your father is perfect, he left us, but you still want him

I hate that my love is not good enough for you

I hate that I've searched deep and wide within myself to right my wrongs, to no avail

Do you know that I too hate how we are?

I hate that most nights I don't sleep, thinking of where we went wrong

I hate that when I decide to come around, I talk myself out of showing up

I hate that in my mind, this will never be

I hate some of the things we went through

And I know you don't believe me, but I hate that I didn't always protect you

I hate mirrors now because I only see me for what I did to you

I swear, I hate that I can't go back

If I could, I promise you wouldn't hate me

Because I wouldn't let my hate filled heart hurt you

I really hate where we are

And I would hate it even more if we died before we tried

So; lets transform our hate into love

"Today is one of those days when I wish I was a little

girl and could climb into my mother's lap

and cry until the hurt goes away."

-unknown

I'M SO FULL

Today is one of those days where I need to curl up in your bed, lay my head in your lap, and pour out my heart. I'm full today. Your grandchild's teacher has emailed me three days in a row and I think she's just being petty, but don't want to misread the situation, so I really need to ask you what you think. Better yet, I wish you would happen to call, so you could hear in my voice that I need your help.

My plate is so full Ma, and I know yours is too. That's why I decided not to tell you for the real reason I stopped by. I tried to sit and talk with you in hopes that our conversation would eventually lead to you asking how I am. It never did though. I wanted to explain to you how proud you would have been of me this past Saturday. I know you couldn't be there, but I still wanted you to know how beautiful things turned out. Now I'm overwhelmed with what's next, and I don't have anyone who I can really be vulnerable with. I guess I need to be okay with where we are because we just aren't that close.

I was reminded of that when I walked in your house with an upset stomach. As I dashed to your restroom without your knowledge, I overheard your conversation. I heard you share your strategy for dealing with your difficult kid, you said, "Girl you gotta love her from afar". I sat quietly when I realized you were whispering, as if you knew I would have been offended by that. Afterall you didn't know that I had even come in.

For the duration of my visit, I tried to stay focused, I couldn't help but recall your remarks in my mind. "You do love me from afar, is that intentional"? Here I am thinking we're both actively working toward closeness, but if this is how you feel, what's the point?

I swear I could use my mother right now. It hurts when you find out that those closest to you, are equally the furthest away. It's painful when you seek comfort from your source of disdain. I don't know why I keep coming here only to see that you could

really care less. I'm tired of hearing stories of how Sunday din-
ner went so well yet I never received an invite.

Excuse my rant Ma, I'm just so full.

"Things are as they are, we suffer because
we imagined different"

-Rachel Wolchin

MY TEACHER

Daughter, you question me

Not with your mouth, but with your eyes

They are mirrors of my imperfections

When I look at you, I see my younger self

Before my innocence was tested by the woes of life

When I try to embrace you as my baby girl

My inner child gets jealous and lashes out

I'm learning how to better respond to you

You question me my love

And not because you intentionally do so

But because you came as my teacher

Initially, I didn't recognize that

I thought you were my rival

"Your influence as a mother is insanely powerful. Be
sure that the advice you give is true & something
you'd yourself try. If not, exercise your right
to say, "I don't know."

-Tierra Banks

JUST STOP

Stop giving me bad advice

Just say that you don't know

I can't afford to make mistakes that cost me more than your pride

I'm not calling you dumb, nor am I saying I'm smarter

But Ma I would respect you so much more if you led me with truth

Sometimes that truth is just you being a listening ear

Sometimes our conversations should lead to prayer and not school

I don't always need you to pour your opinion into my empty
cup

I don't always need to know what you'd do if you were me

You try to judge my choices of friends, like you have good ones
yourself

Or you try and give me relationship advice when you can't keep
a man

I don't want to filter what I tell you out of fear of being criticized
or led astray

I want to be able to tell you everything whether it's good, bad,
or indifferent

 I want to be able to trust that you won't put my spirituality on
trial if I have a carnal moment

I want to be able to laugh with you about mistakes I make

Then have healthy dialogue where you offer good advice

I just want the best for us

But please ma, don't try to be my lord

"Lucky is the woman whose first child is a daughter"

-Prophet Muhammed

DAYDREAMING

One day we will arrive

We will co-exist peacefully within our family

Through trials and tribulations, we will support one another

No matter the distance, we will remain connected

Our hearts will sync

The kicks she once felt while I was in her womb, will become

like the love and laughter exclusively between us

Her soul will yearn to relate to mine

Our mother-daughter bond will be like no other

The pain of our past will be washed away by floods of joy

And our relationship will be mutually gratifying

"Mothers of daughters are daughters of mothers

and have remained so, in circles joined

to circles, since time began."

-Signe Hammer

LET ME EXPLAIN

I'm mad at you because I'm mad at me.

I cannot love me but hate you.

I cannot love her and hate you.

I cannot heal me but wound you.

I cannot trust her but not you.

I understand now.

I can only do for me what I'm willing to do for you.

We are the same.

We are connected.

"A daughter is one of the most beautiful

gifts this world has to give."

-Laurel Atherton

MY DAUGHTER, MY GIFT

Suddenly you entered the world, and that's suddenly as in 24 hours 6 minutes and 21 seconds suddenly. Not to mention the 9 months that I waited for you to arrive. I knew things would be different when you got here. I felt the passion you had as you grew inside of me. I felt the kicks, coughs, and hiccups.

I said "that's my girl" as I imagined who you'd look like and sound like! That's right, I had an idea of the cute little voice you'd have. How I would one day find you in my makeup and my heart would melt as you uttered, "Sorry Mommy". I wondered how I would be stern with my precious mini me. How could I hurt this little angel who resembles me?

I already knew your thoughts- they were like mine. I knew you wouldn't like onions because I didn't. I knew you would love Barbies because I had been saving my over-extended collection of them that your grandmother knew I'd love. And I did love them and so would you. But then, you said you preferred American Girl dolls and I was like, "How did this happen"? I asked myself, "How is she not in love with what goes 3 generations back"? How can she be so honest? After all, I didn't even know if I loved Barbies for real, but I had no choice.

Daughter, how did you get so brave? Who told you that you can choose and decide and even change what you don't like about what I'm giving you? These are our genes baby, don't you understand?

But then this beautiful young lady arose and said, "I love you Ma, but I want to be my own person. Stop making me disappoint you when I reject your blueprint for me".

"But I can't help but recollect what my letters said to you before you were born. I knew you; I know you, I made you" I responded. Suddenly as I stared into my daughter's face, I heard

God speak, "No I made her, then I chose you specifically to deliver her. She has a purpose that only I can reveal to you and her. Just ask me".

That day I realized my daughter was a gift that I got to unwrap but like any other gift, I didn't get to decide what I receive. And that's okay.

"No matter how old she may be, sometimes
a girl just needs her mom."

-Cardinal Meymillod

WHAT I WANTED AIN'T WHAT I GOT

I just wanted to be...

Seen by her

Loved by her

Called by her

Cared for by her

Admired by her

Adorned by her

Esteemed by her

Protected by her

Preferred by her

Instead I was…

Ignored by her

Neglected by her

Silenced by her

Disgusted by her

Abused by her

Manipulated by her

Broken by her

Deceived by her

And still I want to be saved by her

"A daughter is a mother's gender partner, her closest ally in the family confederacy, an extension of herself. And mothers are their daughter's role model, their biological and emotional road map, the arbiter of all their relationships."

-Victoria Secunda

MY REFLECTION

You came from my womb

That makes us womb-mates

We carry the same scars

That makes us wound-mates

Everything I ignored

You must now face

Every marathon I walked

Has become your race

"Dear Mom, I get it now"

-unknown

DEAR MOMMA

I'm sorry I didn't understand back then. I was concerned with what everybody else was going through in their house. They told me their moms were mean, and didn't care for them, so when I came home to no dinner, I thought I could relate. I thought you were tired of being a mother because you said it that one time, I left the eggs in the car and it was so hot they went bad. I didn't know you were just upset because you had spent your last on groceries. If I had known I would've offered to buy some from the store on my way home.

Anyway, I want to apologize because I called you out of your name to my dad. I just knew he was mad at you too for not allowing him to pick me up last time. You were saying it was too late when it was only six o'clock, but now I see that if you would've let him come, I would have been with him that night he was robbed. It was because you knew how careless he was. You knew daddy loved to ride around with a pocket full of money and loud music. "Stunting" as you called it. It's funny now, but I wasn't laughing then because I was furious with you.

Ma I really want to apologize for flipping when you made me get birth control after I told you that I had a boyfriend. I thought you were trying to call me fast because of who I hung with. Granted, my girls were hot, but I swear I didn't realize it would be so hard to remain a virgin. I'm so glad you decided to put me on Depo. I cried when I found out my bestie couldn't go to prom because she was pregnant. That could have been me.

I appreciate you sitting me down to explain how you had me at 16 and how hard it was for you to get by. I had never put two and two together. My fault Ma, I guess you aren't crazy after all. I guess you don't hate me, or you aren't hating on me. For some reason, my teacher suggested you might be jealous of me because you didn't get to graduate with your class. I'm so sorry for letting that negativity divide our family.

#positivevibesonly

"Perhaps one day, they'll understand all the sacrifices

she gladly made out of love for them."

-John Mark Green

HER CUP RUNNETH EMPTY

She's been the Tooth fairy, Easter bunny, and Santa Claus.

Best friend, enemy, and confidant.

Nurse, counselor, and teacher.

Everything in one, everything for everyone.

But everybody blames one, even she blames herself.

All she is, is still not enough.

For her, for him, or for me.

Now she's lost and is no good for no one.

Not even herself.

Holidays past, nights cold, kids grown.

All that performing miracles has tired her out.

All that peace keeping has disturbed her peace.

My love, my momma, what do you have?

What did you keep along the way?

What's yours and no one else's?

What did you buy for yourself while you shopped?

Who prayed for you after you prayed us to sleep?

What boogeyman did you fear?

How hard was it to sleep on an empty stomach?

How cold were you when I had 3 blankets?

Who did you talk to when the phone couldn't ring?

Or what quenched your thirst when the water didn't run?

I never saw Santa kissing mommy, so who loved you ma?

Who held you close like you held me?

52

"The more a daughter knows the details of her mother's life, the stronger the daughter."

-Anita Diamant

I CAN HANDLE THE TRUTH

Please share with me,

all you went through, and how you felt.

I need to know now that I must be what you were.

You made it look easy.

Now I'm confused.

I think it's different,

 I think I have it worst,

but you say I don't.

Some things just aren't adding up.

I need your story,

I need your truth.

"One of the saddest things in this world, is to see a child grow up hating their mother because they never knew her side of the story."

-unknown

SO, YOU WANT THE TRUTH HUH?

Well here it is. I was having fun, young, dumb, and broke, when everything changed. My nipples started feeling tender and my face began to glow. One of the old ladies on my street grabbed me and put two fingers on my neck. She stood as still as a deer, then told me I was pregnant. She said, "she felt another pulse". My daddy was pissed. My momma was too, but she said she wasn't surprised because I was so fast.

I contemplated aborting you. When I told your dad, boy did he flip! He claimed I wanted it to happen, so I was thinking about erasing any remembrance of that night in his car. Like I said earlier, we were having fun. Any who, I later decided, I was keeping my baby. I somehow started to believe that God must have been giving me a gift. I felt good as you grew inside of me and I prepared for you as best I could. One of the neighbors let me work in her store. I saved all my money to get you this sharp bassinet with the lace all over it- it was bad!

Fast forward to your first week home, things were rocky. Your dad scattered, along with all my other girlfriends who claimed they would be there. Even my closest homegirl disappeared, and I made her your godmother. This was our new reality. Grammy and Grandpa passed after a while, all I had was you.

Then your cuteness began to wear off and your mouth got smart. Unfortunately, I held you so tight, you were trying to get away. That reminded me of every other person who used me and left. I was tired of being thrown away like yesterday's trash. So I decided to give up on you before you could give up on me- and set you FREE! It was no longer my concern whether you ate, laughed, bathed or whatever.

I picked my life right up where I left off before you arrived. I found my old friends because I wanted to finish what we started all those years ago. Funny thing is, they were now having kids. Then, I found your dad. That dude had a whole wife and some kids outside of us, but I didn't care, I wanted my man back! I just wanted to be carefree and in love like we were before you popped up on the pee stick. He claimed he wanted me too!

That's just how it happened babe. Back then I didn't realize you were somewhere mad. I thought you wanted no parts of me. I thought seeing you in passing at the house was enough. You didn't seem to enjoy my company and you had plenty of friends to take my place.

Baby I wanted what I thought you had. I know I was the elder, but I envied your life. I didn't know finding me would cause you to lose you. I swear, I never meant to put you through what I went through.

But here we are…and that's the truth!

"A mother is a person who seeing there are only four pieces of pie for five people, promptly announces she never did care for pie."

-Tenneva Jordan

HER-STORY

Before she became my mother, she was a person

She had fingers with painted nails, smooth black hair, and bright white eyes

Her voice was as sweet as her dreams to become a nurse and help save the world

Her car was crumb-less and clean, no fingerprints in sight

It looked as new as the designer bag she treated herself to twice a year to applaud her own hard work

And her weekend plans were as sporadic as her decision to cook a good meal

But then I arrived

And suddenly all her own aspirations evaporated into thin air

She now only saw life through the lens of our family

Her nail polish became a distant memory as she "embraced her natural self"

She no longer did "like" bags, because she traded that desire for the best things her money could buy her children.

By the time I grew up, my mother was a bitter bland lady

She had few friends and a faint spark

Elaborate vacations she had not been taken

Nor had she been on the books of anyone's salon

There was no pizazz, hardly any femininity

The only R and R she knew was recipes and remedies

"Everyone was thinking it, I just did it."

-A Cycle Breaker

THAT'S IT…I'M THROWING IT AWAY

This block does not fit.

I've even tried to build around it, but it just does not fit with the other blocks.

I thought it went there because it blended in like it belonged.

"Who put it there?"

I do not know; it's been there for as long as I can remember.

I inherited all of these blocks.

My mom built with them.

And she said they were passed down to her from her mother as well.

That's a long time.

I have got to get rid of it because no matter what I try to create, it falls.

I can't understand how my mom and grandma built with this thing; it drives me crazy.

"I wonder why nobody ever got rid of it?"

I don't even want it around; it may find its way to all the other stuff I'm going to pass along to my daughter.

She must not even see it; what if it discourages her from attempting to build anything at all?

I just decided.

I'm throwing it away.

"She taught me that fear is not an option."

-Diane Von Furstenburg

A TEACHER INDEED

You taught me to floss my teeth after I ate chicken or corn

And how to shave my armpits smooth as silk

Then I told you I liked boys, so you told me about STD's

And taught me how to put on a condom.

I was scared but I was prepared

Remember you showed me how to wash the baseboards- move

everything out when I sweep and do laundry in one day, you

know; by folding and putting the clothes away as I go

So of course, a clean house is no issue for me

Then you said my sister and I had to be close

If we fought, you would make us hold hands for hours

I hated that…but now I wish I had the heart to ask her to hold my hand

You were right, she is my best friend

On Sundays we went to open houses in the heights

You had us thinking we were moving on up, as we called "bingo" on our future bedrooms

What I didn't know was that you were teaching us to dream, we weren't actually moving

Now that I think about it, my current home is more like those houses than I realized

Thank you for that

You know something else you taught me?

How to try

I watched you try marriage, second jobs, fostering children, baking, befriending and more

When things didn't work, I watched you try again and again

You bought houses, switched our schools- tried private even though we couldn't afford it – wow

You even took us far away as possible, so we wouldn't live through what you did

You tried church and had us baptized early

You even let us try

We tried modeling, cheering, drill-team, high-stepping, driving, working, doing our own hair

You even became a troop leader

Good job Mommy

Thank you for your bravery

Thank you for standing when you wanted to fall

Thank you for smiling when you wanted to cry

Thank you for doing it blind when you couldn't see a way out

That was tough- I understand now

And because I witnessed your sacrifice, I can make my own

I gotta be just as brave as you were, you've passed the torch

It's on me to improve the system

Each generation must do their part

I salute you Queen for doing yours!

"You were unsure which pain was worse – the shock of
what happened or the ache for what never will."

-unknown

IT COULD BE WORSE

Do you think it makes me feel better because it could be worse? Well it doesn't. This is hell if you ask me. Not having a relationship with the one who brought me into this world, is insane! Like, how can you just go on with life without me? How can you smile on holidays not knowing where I am?

I'm beginning to hate holidays. What makes them special is who you share them with it and I'm tired of not seeing you at the table. This is so far off the dream you sold me when I was young. You used to say things would be okay. Is this your version of okay? People always say, "You only get one momma" and that's so true, but I'm irreplaceable as well.

I just don't get how it could be worse. I love you so much and I want you to want me so bad. Sometimes I think of how it would be if you passed. I wonder if it would be easier to cope with faded memories and distant rapport. I wonder if not being able to visit would sit better with me than not wanting to. I've even wondered how I'm going to act at your funeral. Will I cry? Will I feel uncomfortable and out of place? Will people look at me and think I'm faking if I'm sad. It's too much to think about.

It's baffling because I never had my father either, but his absence doesn't bother me nearly as much as yours. It's like I never had him and never expected to. That's not the case with you Ma. I have such a high regard for you. You're superhuman to me and I have high expectations for you. I used to ask myself why I have such high standards, now I see it's because I know what you're capable of. Shoot, if you could just give me what you give everybody else, we'd be good. You support them so eagerly. I watch you. They call for help and advice, you'll stop everything to be at their disposable. I just want that, you know. Nothing special just that. But we both have decided it's easier to create with others what seems too difficult to fix between us.

"Never doubt my love. From the moment you were born, my heart opened wide. Please forgive my mistakes and know I am trying my best. There will be life challenges, just remember we can get through them."

-A Mother

APOLOGY

I didn't know better said mom

It's too late said time

I was right there said she

Were you invisible asked me?

I couldn't face that said her

So, you decided I could hurt

But I didn't decide anything

No, you decided to chase your flings

Daughter hear me I know I was wrong

Ma, please sing a new song

Baby please one more shot

Ma, I promise, I'd rather not

Let me prove I'm here for you

How can I know you'll come through?

 The only way is with your trust

I'll trust God if I must

Whatever you say, I need you dear

Okay mom, I'm right here

"Our only goal as a mother should be to raise children that don't have to recover from their childhood."

-unknown

LOVE LIKE CANDY

Sometimes when I open my mouth my mom speaks. At times when I open my heart, love comes in. It's funny because the love ain't like mommy's love- it's different. Its mushy gushy like candy that kids rave about. Mommy's love was hard like jawbreakers. It started out pretty like skittles but left you bare like when you suck all the color off.

Much like cheap gum that only last five minutes, our conversations were shortly sweet and quickly flavorless. Just long enough to hear her fake "I love you" and "I don't know what I would do without you". When I knew just what she'd do. She left us as quick as those church mints melted. Before you could even notice how sweet she was, she was gone. I remember her coming back and forth every time she had a break-up, but I didn't miss her by then. She reminded me of those sticky dots that got all in your teeth. All that residue that you had to scrub out when you knew it was a bad idea to indulge to begin with.

Y'all wonder why I stay away from candy now. I rather pop mollies because it helps me forget about what mommy did. I'm done crying over a love I never felt. I'd rather numb the pain that she caused. When I'm high I don't complain. So yes, I'm a runner now and y'all can call me crazy if y'all want, but I'm done falling for her games. I don't need her, and I don't want her. I just have to keep telling myself that until I believe it…but who am I fooling…nobody but me.

"A daughter is just a little girl who grows up to be your best friend."

-unknown

THINKING OUT LOUD

It's hard for me to see my friends with their mom's

They laugh, they cry, they have inside jokes

We used to have that

Somewhere it stopped

Somehow you stopped knowing me

And I stopped knowing you

So, we drifted and drifted and drifted apart

Now so much space is between us

I wouldn't dare call us close

I'm not the first person you call to share your good news

We never reach out to each other for help

And when I come around it seems forced

Everybody around you is closer to you than me

You hardly ever visit me or call the kids

I can't even think of the last birthday party you attended

But…

In my dreams, we're BFF's

We go on vacation together

We grocery shop on Saturday morning

We go see chick flicks and cry our eyes out

Our manicurist is the same and so is our gynecologist

The same stylist even does our hair

On our off days, we play board games at my house

When you arrive, you enter with a key

On Sunday evenings, we cook dinner together

Well you actually make everything; I'm just your sous chef

And your grandkids think you're amazing

Not because you tell them but because you show them

You come to most of their concerts and games

Their principal even knows your name

But in reality- we're just not there

"We worry about what a child will be tomorrow,

yet we forget that she is someone today."

-Stacia Tauscher

IN HINDSIGHT

What you needed from me, I never got

So, I thought you'd find your way

Now I see I had things twisted

And you're forced to heal from my parenting each day

I used to frequently call you weak

But only because I thought I was strong

You came to me as you should have; I am your mother

Looking back, I realize I was wrong

"What the daughter does, the mother did."

-Jewish Proverb

TAKING CREDIT

I get so mad when you say, "I'm just like you".

Like what did I do on my own if I'm just like you?

It infuriates me because you only take credit for the good stuff.

You love to claim my successes, but my limitations are or-phaned.

They just happened right?

I didn't learn to hate women from you huh?

Did you forget you told me that they were all phony?

Did you forget I was there when you smiled in your friends faces?

Then you gossiped about them when they left.

That confused me.

Now I can't keep a friend

And of course, you want no parts of my rejection issues.

They didn't come from you either.

So, what about how you rejected me?

When I begged for your attention, you were always busy.

Yea, you bought me toys and "stuff", but for what?

I had no one to play with Ma!

I remember days I wanted to lay with you and just watch TV,

but I couldn't because there was always some man.

You were consoled while I cried myself to sleep.

But not your issue, right?

Now I'm a clingy woman and you want no parts of that.

I didn't get that weak stuff from you, huh?

That must've come from my dad's genes, only perfection came

from you.

BE FOR REAL!

"Either come closer or stay away, having

you in between is very exhausting"

-unknown

SPEARS SHAKEN

To be or not to be is not what I'm thinking

I'm thinking either you is or you ain't

You're either family or you're not

You're either wrong or you're right

You either believe me or you don't

You either see me or you're blind

You either hurt me or help me

You're either forgive me or you don't

You're either trying or you quit

You're either here or you're gone

You either love me or hate me

You're either my daughter or my enemy

Or worse, or better

And either way I'm still here

And that's why to be or not to be ain't what I'm thinking

Because after all this, I am still your mother

"Ain't a woman alive that can take my momma's place"

-Tupac Shakur

MY MOMMA COLD

She could make a good meal out of anything

She can have 7 kids spend the night and nobody gets hurt

Her stories are bomb, her hairstyles are cute

And she knows how to make this little honey stuff that knocks
colds right out, I love her

She can dance, she can pray

She would even come to my school and rep me like when I was
five

My grandma told me that she's been a good girl

How all the boys liked her cuz she wasn't giving nothing up, if
you know what I mean

Mom is cold

She cut grass, shovel snow, change tires and pump gas,

She moves quick when she has to and takes her time when she
needs to

And moves just right when things got to be perfect

She made volcanoes, took walks, cleaned rooms, washed walls

And did laundry all before we got home at four

Daddy always saying, "That's why I married her"

Lucky duck

Man, she even cared about our feelings, bought us journals and
everything

And she respected our privacy

Now I be expecting everybody to love & care how she does…

But they can't cuz my momma cold

"It is easier to build up a child, than it is to repair

an adult… choose your words wisely"

-unknown

I AM NEEDY

I am needy and so are you

Everybody is

You've been trying to convince me that it's just me who you

have trouble with

Like what I'm asking is unreasonable

Well really Ma, all your kids feel the same way

I'm just the one brave enough to speak up

And that's because I'm the one that's outspoken like you

How can you be mad because I demand the truth?

That's respect and all I need is R-E-S-P-E-C-T

If you respected me as a woman, then you would value my opin-

ion

You wouldn't sweep my feelings under a rug

You wouldn't call me boujie or judgmental

I'm not judgmental- I have standards

I have values that I don't negotiate

I learned not to in therapy

You should really try and get to know me

I could share what I've been practicing

Let's break the cycle

I know we can be better Ma…

So, I guess you're right, I am needy

And again, so are you

Truth is, we need each other

"Strong as a Mother"

A MOTHER

A mother does the job that no one else can

No one else can be as immortal, or unbothered as she must be

Her blood cannot shed, her bones cannot ache

Her body does not operate on sleep, food, or water

She receives little pay from her employers,

While praises from spectators are plenty

Her feelings don't matter

There is no grace for her limits

Her heart must be diamond because it cannot break

Her eyes are like a kaleidoscope; things are never as they seem

She is an interpreter

Her dreams are abstract and unattainable

While she actualizes the dreams of others

Perfection is the perception

Mistakes are her kryptonite

She has no guide

She's trained along the way

And receives few tangible benefits for her labor

Her pay is often with words, sometimes nice sometimes nasty

Her pride comes in the form of her loving offspring

Her abilities are evaluated by their success

She must forgive, she must forget, and she must remember

She is the source

And no one besides a colleague could fathom the sacrifice required of her position

Because to understand a mother, you must become one

"We simply can't abandon ship every time we encounter a storm in our relationship. Unconditional love is about weathering the storms of life together."

-Seth Adam Smith

WE'LL GET THERE

I came by today and I prayed silently before switching off my ignition. I asked God for strength to conceal my broken heart. I wanted to greet you with a smile, but I didn't want you to sense my overexcitement to be in your space. I wanted to breathe in your air in hopes to take in your love. I wanted to know what you were doing right before I came. Had you thought of me as you slept? Was I at the forefront of your mind when you woke up?

Now I'm inside. As we try our best to converse, we stumble over our words. We are both trying not to offend. We guard our hearts because the thought of this moment being real is too much like a fantasy. My teeth cringe as you mention others who seem to be able to show you more love than I can. My palms sweat as I muster enough courage to trust you with my secrets. "She is beautiful", I think to myself. As I listen for what you aren't saying, I can see that your soul is kind and soft but hurt. I just want to make it right.

Mommy, I had to leave. My heart started pounding and for a second, I thought we made it. I almost asked you a forever question, but our present state suddenly became a disclaimer. So, I dashed out, ran to my car, slammed the door, and prayed myself off an emotional cliff. I had to remind me that I'm trying and so are you. It's hard you know, because our hearts break and beat to the same rhythm. Suddenly, a small voice whispered, "You'll be fine", Mommy, we will be fine, we will be good, we will be MENDED, I love you!

"But behind all your stories is always your mother's story, because hers is where yours begin."

-Mitch Alborn

I'M PROUD OF YOU

There were no counselors when I was young. I mean there were, but not for girls like me. I didn't realize that I grew up in a dysfunctional environment. I knew there were drunks, addicts, and perverts around us. I didn't know those were sicknesses. I thought all we had to do was survive and that would make us exempt. I thought when you and your siblings stayed sober, y'all were okay. Hell, that was more than I could do.

I'm writing you daughter, not to excuse anything, but to simply let you know that I'm sorry. I'm sorry I wasn't perfect. I hate what you saw and grew up around, and what you had to do to fix your heart. I want you to know that I am proud of you! You inspire me because of your bravery. You sought professional help even after I told you it wasn't necessary. Now I see how important that really was. Thank God you got it babe! You changed our trajectory.

The women after you won't suffer in silence. They won't be lost and confused or ashamed of where they come from. That's what you meant by owning your own story huh? I wish I had the resources you had at your age and for a while I envied that about you. But that's not the case anymore. I thank God that he preserved my lineage. I'm no longer embarrassed about being a part of your struggle. I've been empowered by you my love, and I really want to say thank you for rewriting our story's

"When you communicate from a place of love,

you will appreciate more and judge less."

-Martha & Alexandra

COMMUNICATION

I told you I liked girls and from there you were full of disgust

I told you I felt like I was weak, and you said I must be tough

I told you I was scared to leave but still I wanted to move away

Then you told me I was running from myself and insisted that I stay

I told you that I had big dreams, I wanted to make myself proud

I said I would overcome my fears that I had since I was a child

I told you that I had questions about the God I was raised to know

But all you did was condemn and judge me, ultimately making me feel low

I told you how much I needed you when I made the choice to abort

I told you that I wanted you there when I had to face him in court

I told you how I wanted to die when life became too much to bear

I told you how your lack of support made me feel you didn't care

I told you how much I hated when you made jokes about our past

I told you how much I loved you when you weren't wearing your mask

I told you how much it meant to me when you did what you said you would

And I would tell you so much more if you listened like you should

"If you live for people's acceptance,

you'll die from their rejection."

-Lecrae

STAMP OF APPROVAL

Your approval is law

Mine is subpar

Yours are truth

Mine are flawed

Yours have legs

Mine can't walk

Yours are loud

Mine don't talk

Yours move freely

Mine stay stuck

Yours are blessed

Mine is luck

Yours can save

Mine just cost

Yours will liberate

Mine are lost

Yours are wise

Mine is premature

Yours is confident

Mine is unsure

Yours have evidence

Mine is a myth

Yours are supported

Mines are adrift

Yours are strong

Mine are proud

Yours are limited

Mines a crowd

Yours are welcomed

Mine are dissed

Ma, your approval is law

And I can't seem to live without it

"My mother suffered silently and smiled so no one

could tell. So, if you see me smiling today,

know my mother taught me well."

-unknown

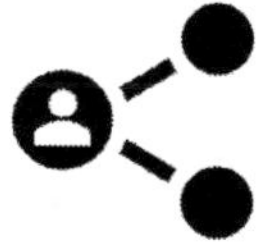

FRAMEWORK

My relationship with you has been the framework of my life. How I love and receive love is based off what you demonstrated. You showed me that I should feel it. Like really feel it. When it's good, my smile shall remain plastered to my face right below my eyes that can see how good it really is. When it's good, I'm good and I should be able to freely soar; I should be confident and able to enjoy all my senses.

When it's bad, my heart shall ache until I can't breathe because if I breathe then I can speak, but while I'm breathless I'm also speechless. And that is what corrupted us. It was the silence that made me lose sight of our victories. The silence makes my inner voice so loud that I am distracted by what's not being said

Our relationship is such an enigma to me. I'm so conflicted with how we went from friends to adversaries. What once looked good and felt better is now affecting other senses like taste and touch. I can only enjoy all my senses when life is perfect. My appetite for nourishment and affection is normal when life is good.

I see it so clear in my relationships now. The same breathless to speechless cycle has corrupted me and many others. It's like I'm a poster child for good but I'm terrible at expressing the other parts. What happened? Why can't I speak through my pain to the one that it matters? What is this mask and muzzle made of that I've worn throughout my relationships?

No fault is found or given to either of us really. You didn't intentionally train me to smile or be silent. Neither did my friends... or my man. Somehow a message was delivered to the inbox of my mind and it's now my default setting. Don't get me wrong, that setting was formed during your reign of supremacy over me. But again, I'm not blaming you. It's just that our relationship is my framework.

See Ma, realizing this has been such a relief. It really liberated both you and me from my arsenal of wrath. As I retrace my steps of assimilation, I can see where the tip of the iceberg had bamboozled me. Here I was thinking I had no place of permanence, when below the surface I was strong and resilient just like you. We were both always looking at an undeveloped portrait. My silence, though appearing cowardice, was simultaneously consideration and confusion. My breathless to speechless cycle was strategic and even though it hurt so deeply to my core, it's how I was formed.

"You can't have a relationship with your daughters until you get a relationship with you."

-Iyanla Vanzant

I'M CHANGING

To be honest, I don't feel bad. I mean I do but life is hard. I won't keep apologizing for what I didn't know. I can't. If I did, it would be a lie because in my heart, I know I did the best I could. It's impossible to make all A's on a test you couldn't study for.

That's what life has been to me; a test. Blow after blow, I had to keep going. There were days all I could do was sit in the corner and cry, pretending to be sleep when you came near. Because that's what it took. I remember days where I had the hardest time making a decision about simple stuff- like dinner.

You'll see babe. Your kids are growing up and I see you tiptoeing over your words, trying to right my wrongs. Letting them be heard because you felt like you were silenced. But trust me, even with all that, when they grow up, they'll have a list of your imperfections too.

That just how it goes. I used to think I was gonna be different than what I saw. And if you ask me, I was but obviously, that difference wasn't enough to win a mother of the year medal. I sacrificed everything for you. I gave up on the things I used to write in my journal since I was a girl. I stopped entertaining the idea that I could be something more than a mom. You may not have had it all, but you damn sure had all of me.

I can't tell you the last time I did something I wanted to do. Every day since the day you were born, I have been on hold. Now holding on to what I don't know, because my slippery hands have let it all go. But I'm just holding. Holding still and holding fast… I'm tired of holding on.

It's my turn to live now. I won't let another second pass where I'm wallowing in regret. These regrets adding up so high that I'm feeling blind and deaf and numb all at the same time. I keep a separate list of regrets for what I didn't do for each of us. Yes, I've let myself down too, but even still your list is winning.

Here's what I decided. I'm going to do you a favor and resuscitate myself. I'm not going to allow you to spend any more of your life holding me in contempt. It's over. I have apologized for the last time and if it wasn't sweet enough, long enough or missing some important layers, feel free to replay it until it sounds perfect in your mind. Maybe your mind is better at making sense of our past than me. Because for the life of me, I don't know why we were dealt this hand. But it was ours.

Along the way, some of those lessons hurt. The pain was unspeakable at times. But I dare not forget the love, joy, and happiness that we've experienced throughout our journey. It is priceless in my eyes. Probably because we're priceless in my eyes.

I love you my child. And I pray that the rest of our lives can be spent dwelling on that. We can't lose if we focus on our love. Now I know I have some work to do and I'm committed.

Therefore, I've reprioritized and this time I'm going to get me together. I'm going to heal and live, love and laugh. I'm going to search my own soul for what lies deep within. I'm going to confront my own fears and take my own risks. They'll be days ahead where I just stare in the mirror and study my reflection.

Making changes is what I plan to do. Uprooting and dismantling the dysfunction in my heart. I will live babe.

And when I start living, I'll be better for you. You'll always be a beneficiary of my discoveries. My scattered pieces will all come together and liberated we both will be.

Daughter promise me you'll enjoy the front row seat of my reproduction. There, all your questions can be answered about who I really am. As you begin to understand how I came to be, don't ever be discouraged by what's revealed. Remember to always focus on our love. Our unconditional love is the only thread that can weave all this together.

By now, I hope it's clear to you that I've moved beyond the mistakes of my past and from the bottom of my heart, I invite you to do the same.

FINAL THOUGHTS

Thank you so much for reading my book. If you're anything like me, this journey through my story was an emotional roller-coaster. This relationship is like that though. One day you're madly in love with your daughter and she is completely inspired by you; other days the two of you can't even share the same air.

I get it. Especially now that I'm a mother. My daughter is my daily reminder that my mother did the best she could and sometimes in her humanness, got it completely wrong.

Before you go, I'd like to reiterate one thing: *PLEASE COM-MUNICATE!* Go talk to her about all those emotions you just felt. As you can see, sometimes she had no clue how her choices affected you. Do not keep it bottled in any longer. That unexpressed hurt has distorted your view of love, life, and loyalty. Trust me- that's not how God wants you to live!

P.s. Whatever she can't accept, leave with Him. Forgive her anyway, whether she's dead or alive!

Made in United States
Orlando, FL
18 March 2024

44896548R00072